A Wreath of Down and Drops of Blood

THE

POETRY
SERIES

A Wreath of Down and Drops of Blood

POEMS BY ALLEN BRADEN

THE UNIVERSITY OF GEORGIA PRESS
Athens & London

Published by The University of Georgia Press
Athens, Georgia 30602
www.ugapress.org

Designed by Walton Harris
Set in 10.5 on 15 Minion Pro
Printed and bound by Thomson-Shore
The paper in this book meets the guidelines for permanence and durability of the Committee on Production Guidelines for Book Longevity of the Council on Library Resources.

Printed in the United States of America

14 13 12 11 10 P 5 4 3 2 1

Library of Congress Cataloging-in-Publication Data

Braden, Allen.
A wreath of down and drops of blood / Allen Braden.
p. cm. — (The VQR poetry series)
ISBN-13: 978-0-8203-3474-5 (pbk. : alk. paper)
ISBN-10: 0-8203-3474-X (pbk. : alk. paper)
I. Title.
PS3602.R339W74 2009
741.5'973 — dc22 2009024823

British Library Cataloging-in-Publication Data available

In Memory of My Parents

KATHERINE BRADEN

&

JACK A. BRADEN

"There is no excellent beauty that hath not
some strangeness in the proportion."

— FRANCIS BACON

Contents

Acknowledgments

My most sincere thanks to the editors of the following publications for publishing these poems, some in slightly different forms:

Bellingham Review: "Flight Theory," "Reversal"

Georgia Review: "The Hemlock Tree"

Laurel Review: "Crew Cut," "Smudge Pots"

New Republic: "Taboo against the Word *Beauty*, Elegiac Version"

Nimrod: "Bird's-eye Maple (*Acer saccharum*)," "Tree of Heaven (*Ailanthus altissima*)"

North American Review: "Grinding Grain"

Poetry Northwest: "Your Life As Found in a Toolbox"

Prairie Schooner: "Taboo against the Word *Beauty*, Epistolary Version Riding the Chicago Loop," "Taboo against the Word *Beauty*, Invocation," "Taboo against the Word *Beauty*, Troubadourian Version"

Seneca Review: "Hubbard's Falcon"

Shenandoah: "Almanac Magic," "Litany Ending with a Taste of Nectar"

Southeast Review: "Taboo against the Word *Beauty*, Version Planted in Sorrow's Orchard"

Southern Humanities Review: "Remembering Precious Landscape, but with an Elegy in Mind"

Southern Review: "Pomegranate," "Refinishing"

Subtropics: "Catalpa (*Catalpa speciosa*)"

Virginia Quarterly Review: "Detail of the Four Chambers to the Horse's Heart," "First Elk, 1939"

Water-Stone Review: "Taboo against the Word *Beauty, Ars Poetica*"

Witness: "Elegy in the Passive Voice," "Taboo against the Word *Beauty*, Premonition"

"Crew Cut" was reprinted in *Spreading the Word: Editors on Poetry*. "First Elk, 1939" was reprinted in *Best New Poets 2005*. "Taboo against the Word *Beauty*, Version Planted in Sorrow's Orchard" was reprinted online at *Poetry Daily*. "Grinding Grain" was reprinted in *Family Matters: Poems of Our Families* and *Naugatuck River Review*. "Litany Ending with a Taste of Nectar" and "Your Life As Found in a Toolbox" were reprinted in *Arbutus* and *PoetsWest*. "Your Life As Found in a Toolbox" was reprinted in *In Posse Review*. "Taboo against the Word *Beauty*, Premonition" was reprinted in *Pontoon 10, Jump Start* and *The Musculature of Small Birds*. "Hubbard's Falcon" was reprinted in *Jump Start*. "The Hemlock Tree" and "Grinding Grain" were reprinted in *Poets of the American West*. "Bird's-eye Maple (*Acer saccharum*)," "Refinishing" and "Taboo against the Word *Beauty*, Version Planted in Sorrow's Orchard" were reprinted in *Floating Bridge Review*. "Refinishing" was reprinted as a broadside by Egress Studio Press. "Detail of the Four Chambers to the Horse's Heart" was reprinted in *Cadence of Hooves: A Celebration of Horses* and as a fine letterpress pamphlet by Peasandcues Press.

Special thanks to the National Endowment for the Arts for a creative writing fellowship, to Artist Trust for a literature fellowship and a Grants for Artist Projects (GAP) award in literature, and to the Dorothy Sargent Rosenberg Memorial Fund, all of which financially aided the creation of this collection. Thanks also to the Poetry Center of Chicago, the School of the Art Institute of Chicago, and Centrum in Port Townsend for providing residencies during which part of this collection was written.

Profound gratitude to Greg Sellers, Judy Galbraith, Barbara Taylor, and Martin Taylor for being there from the beginning; to John Wood for teaching me how to live in a world of arts, ideas, and passions; to Dan Daly and Amy Fleury for their perseverance and their poetry; to Joseph Green, Kevin Miller, and Derek Sheffield for their Old Town wisecracks and wisdom; to Marlene Bosanko, Sue Ford, Tamara Kuzmenkov, and Alan Waugh of Tacoma Community College for their advocacy; to William Trowbridge for his encouragement; and to my sisters for a lifetime of unconditional support.

A Wreath of Down and Drops of Blood

Taboo against the Word *Beauty*, Invocation

Hear me O Muse! Dictate tricks of the trade:
            words rare as blue-hoofed mare or black-
mouthed whelp. Prove that salt burns sweet,
            bruise preludes bliss, nettles the blistering

kiss I'm mad for. Bite my tongue, nurse
            its wound with pine pitch. *Psych!*
Dirty kneed and flirty, lick yourself clean,
            more or less a slutty possum dozing

in my crawlspace. The *Union Beautific* nightly
            clobbering your possum lovers dumb.
Take my hand and walk these tracks: no sublime
            marsupial heaven of endless pantries,

no beauty sings. Slake this godforsaken thirst.
            Hold your breath. Your turn to play dead.

Smudge Pots

He's not going to live forever,
says the dash light that blues his face.
On a dare he hits a switch:
gone are the high/low beams
and the road's broken yellow
strafing by, only a black gap to aim for
between orchards of scattered light.

Only these pots ablaze with diesel
and the cold glow of gauges
are brighter than the frozen spell
cast over the sky. High on fumes,
we fly by the budding limbs half-radiant,
half-smudged. The studs of tires
click over concrete like static on an LP.

Tonight a typical Saturday night:
those girls at the Lariat Drive-in
tricked burgers and fries out of us
with the magic of their slick Levis;
my friend said, *I get the blonde*;
then home through the sequined dark
to dream of a girl who sighs, *Always*.

Taboo against the Word *Beauty*, Epistolary Version Riding the Chicago Loop

Dear Kevin:

The elevated train's not called "El" but "L"
As in *Lucky*, *Lonely* or *Love*. In a posh bar
Beauty kept reaching across her husband
To stroke my arm. They'd been married
Long enough he didn't mind or notice.
No kidding about love on Dearborn either.
"Give with your heart, not your wallet."
Seems everyone on the street has needs:
Spare change, sponsor a child, hold me.
One man shows me the scar on his face.
A knife fight in prison. He knows I have
Mercy. Anymore, he's that pane of glass
Detached from Walgreens' windowsill.
I look through it. Then step around.

Take Good Care, Allen

Flight Theory

What makes the chimney swift approach the sky
Is ecstasy, a kind of fire
That beats the bones apart
And lets the fragile feathers close with air.
Flight too is agony,
Stupid and meaningless.

— JAMES WRIGHT

His only desire

to do with her body
what air does to a feather.

— JAMES BERTOLINO

The barn swallow knew
                                        all of her eggs
but one
            would be obliterated.
After death, when one of her talons
was carried into the fire ants' den,
that swallow lived again.
                                        Certain consolation
spells agony. Just ask the Puritans.
Such was not the case
                                        for a hummingbird
that blundered into particle board
newly raised in its flight path . . .
stiletto beak
impaled inches deep.

For the Museum of Natural History and Wildlife,
workers jig-sawed around the limp body.
Everywhere
                    the same story spreads
its wings.
I'm talking about the police chief
shooting down a heron.
                                        Right there
at Main and 1st.
That was Grandview I think.
Or Prosser. *Could have been*
anywhere.
                  It was something to do.
Something for small town humdrum.
Locals argued
                         which special-interest group
would be first
                         to take offense.
I'm talking about the gulls and crows
wheeling above a tractor
ousting nightcrawlers and gophers
into the open. The birds dove
                                              and swallowed,
their shitting so bad
the farmer constructed a flail:
a broomstick with baling wire
did the trick.
                        You wouldn't believe
such hardship. A woman I loved once
loved me the way girls want horses.
It's true
              but not what I'm saying here.
Naw, not quite.

I'm talking about seasons
of owls smothered in the granary.
Bet there's more to that story, eh?
Can't drive through the countryside
without dead crows dangling from fence wire.
Be clever: Say murder. Say it!
Tonight's sunset like the sheen
on John James Audubon's
                    dissection table.
Ha! More like love spread-eagled against a wall.
An evening full of starlings
pouring through the air like unchecked water.
I held her, and we witnessed,
                    still no closer
to comprehension.
How many nights did I try
to retrace the complexities
of starlings with my hands over her skin?
I've double-checked the pica and font.
I've got my theories.
                    Story of cruelty
without meaning,
how is it you always insinuate
yourself among these syllables?
Audubon killed what he loved best.
Come on, don't look so
surprised. A story has to start somewhere.
I'm told on his mantel Vermeer
kept a flute
          carved from a swan's wing bone.
Nothing knows the wing like wind.
Let's pretend the first angel
throttled a white swan for its wings

and its nest
in our hearts.
Tell them Wm. Blake sketched his wife
and sang to her for an hour,
then dropped dead, and that's a fact.
Dear metaphor,
let down your hair for me,
put on your black silk,
your best
"come hither."
Don't fail to fall off the tongue.
Beautiful. God! Yes!
Fruit is bound to rot
and flies descend.
Wave them off,
they return.
Persistent as sperm.
I'm talking about that summer
the syllables,
multitudes of them,
darkened the sky above us.
If I ever see her again,
I'll speak
of pebbles transported south
in the crops of a million birds.
Tell them, will you?
Okay, okay. A feather rests
on my windowsill,
and when the baseboard heater
kicks on as I write this,
that feather dances
a little.

Taboo against the Word *Beauty*, Plagiarized Version for My Ex

Baby Doll, consider how our lust was spent.
Reckon your pilgrim soul. Of its whereabouts,
Be wary. Straighten up and pledge allegiance
To Audioslave,

Not Eminem. Check out this symbolism.
Your little wren of a heart bustles its wings—
Beauty, beauty. I nose-dive into your nest,
Scarfing down fledglings.

All that's stark and all that's tight meet in your as-
Pect and between those thighs. If ever two were
None, then surely we should've bowed down to Gen-
X love gods, repent.

O for a beak full of your warm south! Bless you
And your sweet demons.

Remembering Precious Landscape, but with an Elegy in Mind

Nevertheless the front yard, even the hawthorn,
flourished. Various roses built a windbreak,
all the catalpa petals splayed themselves open,
and pollen splotched the limbs in gold profusion.

Suppose a woman lived there, a young wife,
her tanned arms dappled from whitewashing,
beautifying the wagon-wheel fence assembled
out of last century's rumbling west for a better life.

Say years later, while kneeling in her rose and iris bed,
she happened to gaze toward the east forty
and witness the men in her family, at a distance,
circling and swinging their long-handled shovels.

They could've been mistaken, a hundred years earlier,
for threshers slapping chaff from the harvest.
They were in fact clubbing a wounded badger,
winnowing its blood into the furrows of stubble.

Now suppose that the irises have grown
wooden, their blues and pinks blackened.
Razed down to the quick, her roses
promise to return. Prolific. Invasive.

Taboo against the Word *Beauty*, Troubadourian Version

Love is so short, forgetting is so long.

— PABLO NERUDA

There ought to be a law against Henry.
— Mr. Bones: there is.

— JOHN BERRYMAN

My life without your love: everywhere
the chalk goes, something's left behind.
On the other hand, antlers dropped by deer
are loved down to nothing by porcupine.
In spring, they say, a young man's fancy turns
to *this*. Meanwhile the swollen Green River
uncovers record snowpack in the mountains,
plus the latest fancy of a serial killer.
Why test your notion of romance by limitations
to skin and bone? A lace of fascia warm
as gentle love when flesh is splayed open.
Disrobe and clothes forget their human form.
I'd cinch a cord around your throat and take
you from behind. I'd do it for beauty's sake.

Crew Cut

The barber says he never did love her
without ever using that word.
Behind a stripe screwing up the pole as if by magic,
his scissors lisp *bitch bitch bitch.*
My father and the other married men,
some for the second or third time,
nod and pocket their fists.
The clipper strips my eight-year-old skull
until it's stubbled as a new beard.
Over the *grrrs* of the razor
he tells them — no — tells us the lies
she bewitched the court with,
the demands she put on him.

Once his work is done,
I bristle like a man's supposed to,
step down and take my father's seat.
The curls of hair drift to the floor.
Snapping his sheet for us
like a magician's cape,
our man is ready
to close and perform his story
for happy hour next door.
Father pays up. He'll go home,
even though the chores are done.
He'll take me back to his wife
and try hard for the right words.

Hubbard's Falcon

Though these words are most likely
For a peregrine, I cannot help feeling
Drawn to names such as *Falco*

Columbarius or *sparverius* to heighten
Lyric, an attempt to moderate those
Notions of which men are capable.

By men I admit to mean you and me,
Those of us governed by the same
Irrepressible science that led

Our forefathers to stone certain birds
And split them open to study the way
Their future coiled inside dark flesh.

But what possible good can come of this,
Someone spoiling for some such prized
Rarity as forcing a bird of prey down?

What good, a falconer might as well ask
When he finally stumbles upon his bird,
The unhooded light gone from its eyes,

Camouflaged but for a red flag of blood
Unfolding underneath lodgepole pine.
There is no question he must abandon

All of what remains where the feathers
And drying blood already grow
indistinguishable from pine needles and dust,

His task now being that of any survivor:
To tally the lost, to print or chisel names
Across the malleable tablets of memory.

Remember this: with falconry or elegy,
Instructions are conveyed, for mutual good,
On how to release and ascend from the self,

Then a striking and rending in open space
And the inevitable returning with a burden,
A grief to swallow and fuel the living body.

Taboo against the Word *Beauty*, Elegiac Version

How can a halo of vigorous flies
indicate anything but renewal?
The truth — simply beautiful —
what's rotten, nothing more. Tonight
smudge pots repeat no recognizable
constellation. Even blemished fruit,
eaten in darkness, tastes lovely.
Such ripeness dousing the air . . .

In conclusion, we call that wind
once blown over a carcass ripe.
If a body can prove the soul exists,
then flesh is narrative. The spirit, lyric.
Even blood drained serves a purpose.
Even shattered glass will glisten.

Reversal

Resurrection only one word
for whatever revises death

with darkened snow brightening
dispersing itself back into the sky

steer's blood thawing pooling
and maggots percolating

a shimmery rind of flies
almost haloing the entrails

lurching up inside its torso
cavity cinching back around

bitter pasture cud and bile
cutting the dull air of October

and a groan from within
this last utterance first now

four quarters reassembling
at the handsaw's touch

in order to outfit themselves
with that bung-cut one-piece

marbled suit as if forgetting
no gesture once committed

can be taken back can heal
this wound to the throat

The Venison Book

1. Dressing

Once a practice handed down,
sticking its throat now frowned

upon by most sportsmen. Blood
will take care of itself. Just aft
of the breastbone with a blade
three whetted inches or more,

cut and continue as if unzipping
the abdomen which splits open
like a satchel packed neatly
with the contents of a lifetime.

From the unexpected profile
of a liver came Roman prophecy.
Imagine your own portents.
To empty the cavity with ease,

you may tip the carcass downhill.
Take care though not to nick any offal.
Into the next tiny room, carve a portal
when servicing the lungs, the heart

which loves to spoil if left intact.
Sever arteries and windpipe. Remove.
Let the buck's antlers alone,
they'll work as handles later.

Or tie a rope over the skull's base,
a half-hitch around the snout.
Now get your rope or chain out,
hoist over a nearby branch or rafter.

Like a lover's stockings, the hide
tugs off. No need for a knife.
Missed point to call this woods
dressing *undressing*, instead of

hog dressing, rough dressing,
to gut, disembowel, eviscerate.
At last you may separate
the liceless cape and head

from the body if you wish
or saw the crown off its skull.

2. Deconstructing

With sinews and veins stripped
naked of such supple buckskin,

with a hatchet or cleaver,
split sternum, lengthwise,
in two. Pelvic girdle likewise.
Call this the H-bone and crack it

smack-dab down the center
to invent your own alphabet
for dialogue between the dead
and living. What does a blade

whisper to flesh but appetite?
Along a line envisioning the spine,
a hacksaw answers. Other bones
prove easy, especially the hinges

where hooves are defined
from each limb's articulation.
With dead weight, the gantry
squawks. Never you mind

any sound but your own deliberate
breath. Quarter what remains
into shoulders, saddle, haunches.
Identify the use and cut of each:

neck and chuck, flank and shank,
the meaning drained away returns.
Next, wrap each with foil tight
for flavor, then paper against frost.

Cold or salt or smoke cures most
kinds of impermanence for a time.
Treat with an iota of respect.
Collect what you've broken apart

and spoken into being. On thick white
butcher's paper, mark your name.

Taboo against the Word *Beauty*, Version with a Flintlock Rifle Triggered Repeatedly

That crack along the mahogany stock
Recollects the explosive story of a boy,
Loading pure black powder by accident,
Who was blown from this page to the next.

The gunpowder, on the other hand,
Alleges a true and contrary version,
Same as the barrel forged in the past
Perfect tense. Like spilt salt thrown

For luck, lead buckshot once peppered
The frozen air of innumerable autumns.
Coveys brought down or snowshoe hares,
Their stories slung onto the table one by one.

Other times the hammer struck its flint
To spark the blood in words like *feud* or *war*.

First Elk, 1939

There's Al Knoll and O. L. Hesner next to the carcass,
my father at eighteen and Uncle Tillman farther off.
Julian Sommers too, odd man out in a raccoon coat
more accurate for downtown's Post Alley
than somewhere above Devil's Table in the Cascades.
This bull elk they bugled into range, then fixed to the hood
of a Model A coupe, was what the camera's lens
had brought into focus and kept whole for over sixty years:
the seven-point rack not yet hacksawed off
to adorn the bunkhouse back home in the valley;
the four quarters, the haunches and shoulders, not yet stripped,
soaked in a barrel of brine and cured for winter;
the prized teeth not yet gentled out of the jawbone
to pretty the watch chain of any pinstriped Mason.
Some, my father says, seem meant for slaughter,
for nothing but a slug in the head and a throat slit
to drain gallons of blood from the ready meat.
The occasion scrawled upon the picture frame is certain.
Otherwise the war would have revised the scene:
Tillman and Hesner on tour in the South Pacific,
uncertain whether only they were meant for beaches
strewn with shrapnel, wreckage, and billowing smoke.
My father is, after all, no bigger than my thumb,
no more noteworthy than any of the others
except the camera captured the likeness,
for a moment, of the man he would become.

Taboo against the Word *Beauty*, Premonition

I have to tell you about the barn owls
caught every winter between our silos
in a hopper for grain pulverized into flour.
Before dying they squeezed in through a vent

that would have been screened up
except for the old man's greasy itch
to lay his hands on something beautiful
or wild. Better yet, both. To swipe the best

wing feather for the hatband of his Stetson.
To nail the bird by dead wings on a hewn joist
or string up feet-first above the salt lick,
the bucket of bone meal, the rat poison.

Its expression in rigor mortis pinched,
the face convulsive as if ready to cry out.

Detail of the Four Chambers to the Horse's Heart

1

Listen. The last time I saw my father
alive, he spoke of horses, the brute geometry
of a broken team in motion. He tallied
the bushels of oats, gallons of water
down to the drop each task would cost.
How Belgians loved hardwood hames the most.
Give them the timber sled at logging camp
any day, the workable meadows in need
of leveling, tilling, harrowing, new seeding.
We could've been in our dark loafing shed,
cooling off between loads of chopping hay,
the way he carried on that last good day.
With the proper encouragement, he said,
they would work themselves to death.

2

Drifts of snow up to their hocks and knees,
the team struggles. They want nothing more
than to droop in the breath-warm barn,
to fill both cheeks with the chopped timothy
of June's first cutting, to muzzle trough water,
then rest. Nothing more now than to rest.
Snowflakes alighting on their hot withers
vanish. The sledge so laden with slush and ice.
They snort, toss, stamp, and fart to keep blood
thrumming through their bodies, heavenly
machinery in sync with work and weather.
Because the driver, my father, chirps and barks
in a barely human way, they labor.
The work will stop when he says so.

3

Breaker of mustangs and broncos, saint
to all things unbridled, you knew cancer
(like the roots dismantling your culvert)
would have you drawn and quartered.
The stallions whipped to sunder limb
from perishable limb. Divided, the evil
in a body loses its power. The fallen
horse, for example, you saw trampled
had disappeared overnight, scattered
across acres by coyotes or not as dead
as you thought. His harem of mares
soon another's. You were often called
a man even then. Name it fate or omen.
Their hooves almost touching the ground.

4

So much can spook a horse when his world
stirs awake: an unlatched gate the wind
knocks, a pine knot popping like a shotgun
in the campfire. If blinders fail to block
all fresh deadfall along his usual trail,
he'll snap the trace. Now loop a rope
around his upper lip to put a "twitch" on.
This, somehow, settles him down more than
the doubletrees' clink and creak, the routine
caress of your currycomb, the molasses
that glues oats in hunks of giddy bliss.
Given sweets, any horse will follow you.
Whisper what you want to this one.
Never question that disquieted heart.

Pomegranate

Consider this Asiatic fruit with only enough flesh
to feed a myth. It would be too easy to mention
Persephone's ascent from the memorial darkness

and up that stairway of her famous misfortune,
a girl clutching a few seeds to her repentant heart,
too easy, though it is spring and this is an elegy.

It would be more appropriate to point out
how the fruit is chambered into four tiny rooms
like those of the heart, rooms crowded

with seeds the shape of tears or corpuscles
that ebb falteringly through a woman's wrist.
It would be best to pause a moment and say

how the fruit of this tree beyond the ocean,
far beyond the confines of her expected life,
holds a name undoubtedly worthy of praise

in this valley of the everyday she calls home,
domain of cup and milk and soap and dishrag,
of spool and needle, cotton ball and ashtray:

forthright but run-of-the-mill these names,
one for a tray to hold ashes flicked or fallen,
another that cloth to wipe the silver clean.

Taboo against the Word *Beauty*, Pastoral Version

So what if trains jostle our apples down?
If light that ripens *each* turns *every* brown?

The solution waits in unfallowed pasture
famous for twitch and fly buzz. It nickers

and stomps to taste a windfall. Gun shy
but wise to whip snap, it wallows in plenty

of dust. Meanwhile the equation inside
our blood, it strives to qualify our dying:

the crossties, rails, and spikes that guide the train
no longer are consumed. What perfection

to feel the sugared apple sweetly crackle!
Our bodies, the only fruits that bruise then heal.

What if this dust is really a ghost arriving?
If elegy's for the dead, what's left for the living?

Elegy in the Passive Voice

Because there will come a time
to straighten up and step inside
every father's blue-collared life.

Because hardly any man alive
is the kind of man a father believes
his son will be, the kind satisfied

to know his future's on a hoist
overhead like a side of venison
that sings the slang of men.

Hook and *work.*
Sweat and *meat.*
Twelve gauge and *trophy.*

Words easy on the ears
but not the tip of every tongue.
Because there are rows of desks

waiting for some resemblance
of truth, for the son to glimpse
a glamorous future all his own,

now old enough for the burden
of men, memories weighed down
with the history of forgetting.

Refinishing

And why not approach figuratively the past
as metaphor ingrained in the here and now?

Peel away the chapped, sun-blistered paint
and shellac meant to simulate rosewood,

the metallic scent of ancient salmon
that literally saturates this afternoon,

that conjures some notion of slender smoke
scrolling up the arc of a welder's blue spark.

Why not resurrect the spangled blood
from that scent, the sockeye revived

from that blood, the unfathomed dark
from that fish? Or why not reconstruct

the crisp lumber from this tackle box,
the tree trunk's girth from the planks,

and even the earth out of which the tree
thrust forth? Strip it down. Begin again.

Taboo against the Word *Beauty*, Answer Key

If a magpie alights on a snowdrift, is it only
half a bird? The answer the difference between
night/day. Bonus: a silhouette of said magpie
conjuring up one angelic/elegiac wingspan.

If a stand of rose hips seems a cathedral
to pheasant, then hypothesize the fox
is hunting again. Rings on the raccoon tail,
around the pheasant throat, the blowfly thorax;

a pearl of gristle on the raptor beak; or lastly
that blowfly burbling circles in a goblet
of poisoned wine . . . proof of life everlasting
or the difference between prophet/poet?

Thus truth, like beauty, may vary. Partial credit
for "the soul is a hive whose honey will not last."

Taboo against the Word *Beauty*, *Ars Poetica*

The poem, someone says, *is a pheasant rooster,*
as if gizzard pebbles were syllables. Feathers, lines.
Once, it was chaff spangling the gleaner's wind.
Less your horse than her reflection in a water

trough, being neither flesh nor bone. No ghost
rattling your shutter, no jangle of bridle. Not even
a hawk spiral, mouse tweet. Say *quartzite* or *obsidian*.
Taste the igneous language? I unearthed its first

desire where your soul's honey lasts and lasts.
Ah, I forget myself. Beauty a lame excuse for love.
It's ice, someone says, *that sizzles on a woodstove.*
More like the tinder: now flame, now smoke or ash.

Instead, the poem has always been an open window.
What could blow in or out today God only knows.

The Hemlock Tree

Did I mention that last night an owl swept down
from her perch in the hemlock nearby
to devour a wild dove tamed by Safeway birdseed?
Of course I can reconstruct the scene for you
from knowing how this testimony
beyond the limits of your city implies the inevitable
circuit of hunger, from knowing how all life must
enter into a kind of covenant with nature
for the living shall consume
                                        the flesh of the living
and from the delicate evidence at hand:
a wreath of down and drops of blood.
And right now you might be wondering
about the wisteria spiraling up that hemlock,
inching a bit higher with each passing year,
offering loveliness in powder-blue clusters
for a few weeks of May, and all the while killing
the tree with its gradual, constrictive, necessary beauty.

Taboo against the Word *Beauty*

Never speak of the orchard's aching abundance,
the glimmer of splintered glass, the auger that funnels
a silo empty. Does it matter what happens

to a paw severed? The coyote yowls
but still outruns the trapper, a metaphor
to show (*not tell*) what one may call

necessary. *Hush now*. Drop a feather
over open flames that set the smoke
free from timber. *Shhh!* Ever wonder

about the nature of beauty? Try to ask
the fire why the feather always lifts,
the falcon why it tears the meadow lark.

Whatever the whetstone imparts to the knife,
all the more reason to release your life.

Your Life As Found in a Toolbox

Everything necessary to maintain
every foundation ever built so far
is found simply by fondling the latch,
easy as recalling a less-than-fond past,
and then by handling each orderly tray
of tools too simple to call hand tools:
a stick of chalk meant for marking
the measure of almost anything
from concrete to an assortment
of planks sorted out as useless;
that yellow Stanley measuring tape
used to measure what used to matter;
and one lead stone to plumb the line,
much like a fisherman's sinker or fob,
and gauge the point of vanishing.

Reach much deeper to find those
that fit the hands perfectly
of any man who constructs
a reluctant living with his hands:
the square a clumsy boomerang
perfect at setting the record straight;
a claw hammer meant to hammer
whatever it can to your expectations
then claw them apart on second thought;
and finally, ultimately, the spirit level
with its single, jaundiced eye
leveled expectantly in your direction
and rolling whenever you breathe,
the only bubble in the world
that won't burst at the slightest breath.

Grinding Grain

The belt, tight as a razor strop,
whips from tractor to hammer mill
and scares out of our grain bin an owl.
Welded pipe coughs flour into bags

stenciled *H & H* or *Logan's Feed & Seed.*
I take another off my father's hands,
another cinched with his square knot
better than any I used to tie.

Easily I buck those bags onto the stack
that shoulders the granary wall.
The air thickens this morning light
sifting around the blurred belt.

When I turn back, he's gone
inside a cloud bank of flour
the way burlap can swallow
so many pounds of ground durum.

All our lives we work this way.
He sacks and ties.
I lift and stack.
Our bodies slowly growing white.

Taboo against the Word *Beauty*, Postmodern Postmortem

Unless beauty's a nest of mice staking claim
to upholstery abandoned, the anonymous
tuft snagged on barbed wire or a tom named
Hope whose sixth toes keep him atop the ice

and snow (worst blizzard any soul can recall);
unless a honeyed carcass jizzes up some parable
of value or draft horses ditch the gristmill
for the range, this numbskull poet feels terrible

(useless unless heartbroke). His brain posted
against trespassers and poachers. Tell you what,
his number's up at last. Organs honeycombed

from elegies unforgiven. Heart like a stove-
up sump pump. Critics say he gave his left nut
for beauty, for one more dark loving poem.

Almanac Magic

for John Wood

Believe in the bounty of drought,
of fire and locust. Count on
jackrabbit luck to grow your seed
and the tip of a dipper for rain.

If the man in the moon is late arising,
and your wife swells with your future,
she'll be craving clay and kneeling down
to eat that dirt from the root cellar.

But know your future will grow up
to leave you, to follow the magpie
with a song of honey and foil
from city neon alive in its eyes.

You stay to plow through days of sod and rock
and pray the rusty dray outlasts the harvest.

Let the wild oat drill into your hands
crooked from handles of shovels and hayforks.
Read your future in the cracks of this land,
in the bumble of tumbleweed and the stir of the hive.

Now listen for wind to shush your wheat asleep
and the scythe as it whispers its name to the sheaves.

Taboo against the Word *Beauty*, Circular Version

A mouse nibbles on spilt seeds

so within her a garden begins

          treat for some owl one day

she drops to earth a bolus the next

          trilobites crawled ashore so fins

could be wings   flames concoct

radiance out of driftwood so tides

haul more in from the horizon

          so far as larvae are sublime

in the eyes of botfly   so a tomb splits

if sperm pierces an egg or moon

          swallows nest where they please

and chirp a worm to bits and pieces

          open a song just so notes live inside

Taboo against the Word *Beauty*, Brief Version Full of Grace

Take, for instance, an earthworm
toiling under a furrow in its dim room,
the swarm licking summer pollen

to warm the stanchioned hive,
or honey warping barn plank.
Still piss-damp, slick and rotten,

the dairy's loading chute echoes
thousands of Guernsey flanks
burning through milk parlor dark

toward the release of colostrum
or slaughterhouse sublimeness.
Forget the time you slapped

a twin calf hard to knock out
its first breath like a prayer.

Litany Ending with a Taste of Nectar

(nek-tar): that which overcomes death

In the one, long, mournful syllable
spilling from the hive hidden in a hawthorn
or the barn's loft emptied of barley straw

In these lilacs redeeming the air each spring
or a cold snap come early distilling
each fist of grapes tugging the vine

In all the fruit, blemished or unblemished,
burdening the never-ending branches
with sugar drawn from orchard sod

In the rose with its layers of numerous
lives: *Fire & Ice, Deep Secret, Heart's Desire*

In pollen held aloft in time like snow
by the photographic disposition of memory

In the son replacing his father,
the daughter her mother, and so on, thus

In the spirit abandoning the body,
wherever there is sorrow, lives what saves us.

Taboo against the Word *Beauty*, Version Planted in Sorrow's Orchard

So many private varieties swell with fruit
or germinate at random within the pods
that no air will stir nor tiny warmth linger.
Catch a glimpse of petals
(white as skull)
easily mistaken for mourning doves.
No birds orbiting these branches now,
not since tinsel trembled in remembrance
of wind or pollen smothered the swarms
administering sustenance.
Consolation
amounts to resin that weeps and fails
to congeal or heal those initials (yours, mine)
emblazoned into bark (corrugated, beloved).
Press an ear against this disfigured trunk
before the pitch of the heartwood perishes.

Elegiac

The turn of centuries or the turn
of a page means the same to me . . .

— AMY GERSTLER

I. Hawthorn (*Cupiditatis*)

for Greg Sellers

First of all, surrender the trees
found in their usual nostalgic landscapes.
Before you proceed
extract
the lovely honey locust, numerous oaks,
the dogwood and schoolyard elms
out of every page.
Here all around the hawthorn's flimsy roots
digger wasps prefabbed
a city in the hillside.
Undermining the tree, yes that's true,
yet preserving the stems, the slender
thorns, and pale clusters of rosettes
from harm.
Maybe you've heard that legend that ends,
And so the King of Winter proclaimed a holiday,
"From this day forward let every limb bearing fruit
be severed."

His daughter had tasted the accursed
fruit grown swollen in their royal orchard.
I'm telling you,
even in slumber she was almost
                                        flawless.
O how the kingdom fell stricken
with grief for this well-favored child.
A hedge of hawthorn eventually
encompassed the castle
                                until some prince
charmed the thorns into softening
for a happy ever-after.
At any rate, Greg,
                        let me start again.
Once upon a hunter, happy on bourbon,
swigging and recounting his limit in the blind,
the breech cracked open across his knee
to cool the barrel. . . . Every loss
                                        renews pleasure
in what remains untouched:
the bagged birds nowhere near
as visionary
as those lifting off
the surface of the Calcasieu.
Wherever the Confederates planted their dead,
for instance, they added a shovelful of lime
to sweeten their sorrow. Consequently
every battlefield prospered.
                                    Okra, oats, tobacco.
You see how much of history leads to grief,

discovery to loss (that serpent swallowing its tail
or a loop dubbing one Old World century
over the last)?

Consequently, a writer
named after this tree warned us:
remove the birthmark from a favorite child,
she dies

of inhuman perfection.

II. Bird's-eye Maple (*Acer saccharum*)

for Ruth Scribner

Here is the imperfect dream of branches and leaves,
some missed opportunity for wind and light,
in order to demonstrate the wood's own notion
of how the work of this grain may be slightly

suggestive of northwestern wilderness teeming
with songbirds by the hundred, bearing witness
to the stripping of bark and the hewing of timber.
Here the fiber itself appears to be faithless

to its origin. Collectively, however, a new pattern
emerges regardless the variety (sugar, paperbark).
An accumulation of defects each like the crescent
on one's shoulder from a childhood inoculation,

each as placental as one long-dormant bud,
one that has failed to awaken for the season,
failed to tender what remittance we expect
of leaves in modest shapes: stars or hands.

We lathe this heartwood down lovingly
and polish with such conviction the surface
translates our reflection into something else
made more beautiful by its own blemishing.

III. Catalpa (*Catalpa speciosa*)

in memory of my mother

How many times must a woman suffer
the children and bury them at this spot
before an unblemished tree sprouts here,

or how many versions of a future miscarry
in order to swing for a spell in the shade
cast by that Indian bean tree? Never enough,

it seems. The riddle's answer another riddle,
how a paper hive dangles on the wind
among such coarsely veined ovate leaves.

Catawba worms and sphinx moths
consume a billion board-feet
per century one bite at a time.

What sort of salvation devours itself?
Might the silhouette found in the puzzle
bark really be the Immaculate Mother's?

Fanatics traveled a thousand miles
to enshrine the yard, the first tree ever
worshipped in the history of our valley,

that is until word spread about the King
of Nazareth's profile galvanized
on a STOP AHEAD sign down the road.

Might we discover some god, revised
with our twenty-first century in mind,
hidden among the sweet embodiment

of catalpa blossoms fragile as scripture?
The sphinx moth finds them delectable.
Maybe it holds the answer with a riddle

scribbled across its powdery wings in
the hand of that god. Emerson grasped
the balance between sacrifice and mystery.

He too had visions of his beloved,
the lost son held only in pitch or pith.
The known fruit of the unknown sweet

enough for that sphinx queen of his.
I know this much of departure, of arrival:
out of sleeping a waking, out of waking a sleep.

IV. Willow (*Salix babylonica*)

for Martin and Barbara Taylor

Whittle this willow down
to wave over the slumbering
unborn three times

no reason for the bough
to weep or snap now
time to praise to glorify

no reason for swampy wind
to awaken Mole & Toad
no reason to fluster a picnic

or detour a journey
no reason for currency
on the tongue to promise

passage across the quickening
river like a rope frazzled
from hitching a barn & house

throughout the blinding
sleet of Christ's Eve
& if the dairy cow refuses

the stanchion for no reason
to birth her breeched calf
welts from a willow switch

spell out all the reasons
to worship every strike
from the master's hand.

V. Tree of Heaven (*Ailanthus altissima*)

for Judy Galbraith

. . . little more than a stake struck into rock

to tether the Great Bull of the Heavens.

For King Gilgamesh, Enkidu left the gazelles

to slaughter that bull. What did he know

of gods and their petty, indecent vengeance?

For the sake of the king, he murdered

the strongest lion, clothed himself with its pelt,

and entered what men named their kingdom,

a foul dark place with fallen trees and stones

in arrangements that confounded his eyes.

O how their love was the deepest of its kind.

For the wild man, the king let his hair go unoiled,

unbound (a cicada leaving one age for another).

Ishtar decreed the city walls would forever

sicken Enkidu: strict rectitude for the bull.

His own wild hair, once as fluid as a crown

of Ailanthus leaves in the breeze and golden

as that of a corn goddess, now darkening

from the fever of the Seven Splendors dream.

Wait. One might think I have lost my place.

Indeed, what's the point of having any king

or savage in a language as new as this?

O how theirs is the oldest of tragedies,

pieced together from tablets of Mesopotamian clay.

And what else could be quite as ancestral

as the Tree of Heaven herself, Great Mother

even to gray Ygdrasil? O this Tree of Heaven

from whose pitch and fruit the ambitious

legions of heroes and angels sprang forth.

For Enkidu's sake, the king placed bowls

brimming with butter, vessels with honey,

appeasements to the Sun for the retrieval

of his friend from the deep currents of fever.

Such was not the Council's will. Not that day.

The wild man died a weakling. The Splendors

vanished. In their mourning the kingdom's

multitudes scraped flint across their scalps,

and those who refused were suddenly revised

into trees rooted wherever they stood,

so I ask you what could be more apropos

anyhow than ending on that which blessed us

with its first so thorough, endurable suffering?

In the end Gilgamesh dreamed that Enkidu

was a stone fallen from the uninhabited sky,

from the bitter halls of Ishtar's kingdom,

which he could not lift, that his body was pure

bronze poured into the ax now at his side

and which split that mighty timber into splinters,

which loosed the terrible bull for its slaughter

and set in motion the stone they named misfortune.

VI. Ash (*Fraxinus*)

for Morri Creech

With a name that evokes one of its own
possible endings, this particular tree instills
a sadness like no other ever written,

like someone who traded an eye for knowledge
of the next land or, in some distant kingdom,
who drank of the hidden well and returned

blinded by a thirst satisfied, by the vision
of a soul enraptured. The village
quaking at the apocalyptic prophecy

of his return. For now don't figure
the song a tragic one. Let it conjure
a warning for children. Never forget

the ruler's head was severed and sunk
in the kingdom's well. Look, the lips move.
What words, Morri? Give the song a name.

Spooked from the orchard by tinsel
wind-shaken, summer birds ascended
in clouds throughout the county.

Later a lightning bolt severed this tree
from the field leveled and harrowed
where it had arisen near a century ago.

What irony in a crown blasted, burnt down
to ashes you considered once, not as trees
but cinders that whispered from the crucible,

mouthing in the deciduous manner of poetry
the unavoidable landscape. Velvet or wafer
ash like rows of crooked crucifixes, the elegiac

quality of moonlight bending these boughs
where a forest of the next century happens
to take root and reach for barren light.

Reconsider the name. Smoke means fire.
Fire, ashes. And so skews any requisite
thread of exposition, hinting instead

how the worst awakens close at hand,
how this tree can thrive only in moonlight
while a dream of fire licks away its heart.

VII. Cottonwood (*Populus deltoides*)

for Amy Fleury

I dreamt that two of them
Sharing a mutual trunk
Were my parents, opposed
Like pages bound at the spine.
Not since Philemon and Baucis
Passed under the temple lintel
Had such untransfigured
Love revealed itself.
Inside the tree's hollow
Core, a newborn hid
Forgotten until wild things
Gnawed through its bark.
You know we don't worship
Any tree like we used to.
We remember instead
Helen's magnificent body
Twisting from a tree branch,
Remember eating our own
Flesh, penalized by a goddess
For felling her sacred grove.
Only the beavers worship
So faithfully, so mortally.
Does this plot ring familiar:
The ditch, creek, or river altered,
Windbreaks burnt far back?
Such well-seasoned words
To pop and crack in sacrificial
Fire. No cottonwood remains

Enough to fuel the imagination,
And every diverted body
Of gully water is not enough
Nor the field of milo nearby,
A false setting for a false story
In which parents, distant
Or near, aren't enough either.
Still, you would say
Redemption is certain:
The more trees felled,
The more likely the light.

VIII. Sandalwood (*Santalum album*)

for Deborah Brink

This, even more than all the others,
holds the darkest of bedazzled light
for the aloe from sandal tree root
enshrouds the Old Testament's dead.
And yet a blessed ax head or saw blade
liberates oil out of such a lucrative heart
that a father need not sell those long ropes
of hair shorn off his wife, his daughters.

If, in the forest, the tree were to fall
out of our kingdom and into the next
without a word or witness, what soul
dare to doubt its inevitable slumber?
If one were to plunge into the sacred
river, this at least would rise and float.

Taboo against the Word *Beauty*, Ornithological Version on Aesthetic Theory

Out of its craw, out of its flimsy trellis
of rib and cords of tendon, out of live flesh
copiously puckered by dark quill darkly
so iridescent,

the red-winged blackbird fashions its art. From wind
shuttling among warm mirages of marsh,
from air sizzling inside its instrumental
lungs, an orchestra

is engineered to orchestrate the thermals
caressing your body just now. Tomorrow?
Yesterday? Neither of sheer consequence here:
climactic moment

of neither coming nor going, when breath ends,
before song begins.

THE

POETRY
SERIES

The VQR Poetry Series strives to publish some of the freshest, most accomplished poetry being written today. The series gathers a group of diverse poets committed to using intensely focused language to affect the way that readers see the world. A poem, at its heart, is a statement of refusal to accept common knowledge and the status quo. By studying the world for themselves, these poets illuminate what we, as a culture, may learn from close inspection.

BOOKS IN THE SERIES

The History of Anonymity
Jennifer Chang

Hardscrabble
Kevin McFadden

Field Folly Snow
Cecily Parks

Boy
Patrick Phillips

Salvinia Molesta
Victoria Chang

Anna, Washing
Ted Genoways

Free Union
John Casteen

Quiver
Susan B. A. Somers-Willett

The Mansion of Happiness
Robin Ekiss

Illustrating the Machine That Makes the World: From J. G. Heck's 1851 Pictorial Archive of Nature and Science
Joshua Poteat

A Wreath of Down and Drops of Blood
Allen Braden

In the World He Created According to His Will
David Caplan